Ashleigh:
God's Miracle Baby

Ashleigh:
God's Miracle Baby

*For with God
nothing shall be impossible
Luke 1:37*

Ramona Antillon

authorHOUSE®

AuthorHouse™
1663 Liberty Drive
Bloomington, IN 47403
www.authorhouse.com
Phone: 1-800-839-8640

First published by AuthorHouse   06/17/2011

ISBN: 978-1-4634-1776-5 (sc)
ISBN: 978-1-4634-1775-8 (dj)
ISBN: 978-1-4634-1774-1 (ebk)

Library of Congress Control Number: 2011909573

Printed in the United States of America

Contents

Prologue.. 3

Chapter 1   The Early Morning Shock 5
Chapter 2   The Horrible News...................................... 9
Chapter 3   The Delivery 11
Chapter 4   First Visit with Our Baby............................ 13
Chapter 5   Ashleigh's Stay in the NICU 15
Chapter 6   The First Time I Held Ashleigh 23
Chapter 7   Ashleigh's Last Month in the NICU 27
Chapter 8   Ashleigh Comes Home................................ 29
Chapter 9   Challenges Caring for Ashleigh.................... 31
Chapter 10   Visits to the Specialty Doctors 35
Chapter 11   Therapy for Ashleigh 37
Chapter 12   No More Medicines for Ashleigh 41
Chapter 13   Speech Class for Ashleigh 43
Chapter 14   Normal Everyday Life with Ashleigh............ 47
Chapter 15   Glasses for Ashleigh 55
Chapter 16   Ashleigh Now... 59
Chapter 17   With God All Things Are Possible 69

Author Biography.. 101

This is dedicated to our miracle baby,
Ashleigh Renea Antillon.

May you always know how special you are! You are truly a blessing in our life. I pray that you will always seek God's purpose for your life and trust what He has in store for your future. God healed you, and you're here for a reason. Always remember who you are. You're beautiful, strong, and smart and made in God's image. There is nothing that you can't do when you put God first in your life. So, go out in the world and testify—let the world see of God's goodness, faithfulness, and healing power! May you touch and bless the lives of people you meet with your incredible story of how God held you in his hands at birth and healed you completely. I pray to God and thank God every day for you. My life has been truly blessed because of your premature birth. We serve an awesome God! Give God all the glory and praise forever!

Love always, Mom ☺

Prologue

On the morning of May 26, 2001, while I was in the ambulance, the paramedic wanted to take me to the closest hospital. I refused. I told him to take me to the hospital my doctor was at, and the paramedic refused. I'll never forget the paramedic on duty that morning. He argued with me a little and was set on not taking me to the hospital of my choice. I insisted that there was no way I was ready to have this baby; after all, I was only twenty-three weeks along. He then looked at me and very firmly said, "Ma'am, if you have this baby now, this baby will not make it!" That's when I agreed to go to Arlington Memorial Hospital. God knew what he was doing; he placed that paramedic on duty that morning. Ashleigh was born at Arlington Memorial Hospital for a special purpose!

Chapter 1

The Early Morning Shock

I remember that the day was May 26, 2001, and the time was about 2:00 a.m. I started to feel really sick, and I was in so much pain. My stomach was in so much pain that it was unbearable. I remember thinking, *It's too soon to be in labor; I'm only five months along.* Since I wasn't allowed to take anything for pain, I decided to just lie down and get comfortable. That didn't work. I kept getting out of bed, having the urge to go to the bathroom. The pain continued. It wasn't until 4:00 a.m. that I called an ambulance to come and take me to the hospital. I had the ambulance take me so that my husband could stay home with our two children, Daniel and Abrianna, who were six and one. I agreed to call him to come get me later, once the kids had woken up. We both thought there was no way I was in labor. But we were so wrong.

The ambulance arrived right away and rushed me to the closest hospital. While inside the ambulance, I remember that the paramedic did everything necessary to treat me in case I was actually in labor. He put IVs in my arm and then used surgical scissors to cut my pants on one side of my leg. All this was so surreal to me; after all, I was only twenty-three weeks. I finally agreed to go to the hospital that he suggested. We finally arrived at Arlington Memorial Hospital in Arlington, Texas. As I was unloaded off the ambulance, I remember feeling scared all of a sudden. The paramedic must have noticed because he assured me that everything was going to be fine and that the hospital would take good care of me. I was rolled into the hospital and signed in at the nurse's station. I was then taken up to labor and deliver and put in an examination room. The nurse checked me, and I had already started to dilate. I was at two centimeters. She asked me if I wanted her to call anyone. I gave her the number to call my husband. I wanted more than anything at that moment to just have my husband by my side. The nurses made me as comfortable as possible as I waited for my husband to arrive. My husband later told me that he came to the hospital expecting to pick me up and take me home. Instead he arrived to hear a big shock: that I was already in labor and delivery and dilated two centimeters! (I guess the nurse who called him didn't go into details.) While I was in the room waiting to be with my husband, I was given medicine to stop the dilating. Later they found out that the medicine didn't help. I remember being scared and wanting my husband by my side. If that wasn't scary enough, then what happened next was. I was given another kind of medicine called Ampicillin, and it turned out that I was allergic to it. The medicine was supposed to help with an infection; instead I had a bad reaction to it. I began to have shortness of breath, and I could feel my chest tighten. I soon wasn't able to breathe. I broke out into a sweat. My monitor went off, and the nurses came over to me to help. They quickly gave me another medicine, which helped me get better. Soon after that my husband came in to be with me, and I felt a whole lot better.

I waited there a little while longer before being seen by the doctor. He finally came to see me and told me that I had an infection called

Group B Strep, which had brought on premature labor. I was treated with more antibiotics to help treat this type of infection so that it wouldn't pass to the baby. I was also given two doses of steroids to help with the baby's lungs in case I had the baby early. It was now noon, and the doctor had raised the amount of medicine given to me in the hopes that it would stop an early delivery. When they checked me again, I had dilated to four centimeters, so clearly the medicine was not working. The nurse told my husband that they were going to try to keep me stable. They wanted to do whatever it took to keep me from having this baby, even if that meant staying bedridden for the next two to four weeks. I was not happy at all! At that moment all I could think about was how uncomfortable I was and how much pain I was in. For one, I had to go to the bathroom in my bed (in a bedpan, of course), and if that's not uncomfortable, I don't know what is. Second, they kept taking blood from the same arm because my veins were too small in my other arm. The tape they used messed up my arm, and I had red marks that looked like carpet burns. I also had big lumps and bruises all over that one arm. I was miserable! That day started out very painful and scary for my husband and me, yet through it all I felt that I was going to deliver my baby very soon.

Chapter 2

The Horrible News

Sometime later the doctor finally came back in the room with us. My husband's mother and father were also in the room visiting and comforting us. Suddenly the doctor began to go over with us everything that was happening. The infection I had could still be passed to the baby, and if I gave birth now the baby only had a 20 percent chance of living. This also meant that if she lived she would possibly be mentally challenged. He then asked my husband if he wanted him and the hospital to do everything they could to help our baby or if he wanted them to do nothing and the baby would die due to the conditions. My heart sank, and I began to cry out loud. My husband then looked at the doctor and very firmly said, "I want you to do everything you can to save her!" The doctor said okay and walked away. My husband walked over to me and began to cry and pray with me. We prayed that it would not be time to have the baby and that the Lord would watch over us and give us strength. I don't know how my husband felt, but it must have been really bad because he even blamed himself for what was happening. Clearly he was not to blame; God had a plan.

Soon I felt peace, even though I didn't understand why this was happening. I knew that God placed me there for a reason and that he would be alongside me every step of the way. God was in control of the situation, and I put all my trust in him. As the hours passed, I lay there in so much pain and discomfort. I was completely bedridden with a band wrapped around my belly that was hooked up to a monitor that let the nurses know if I had a contraction. I hadn't had anything to eat, and I wasn't allowed to eat anything because of everything going on. So I was very hungry. Food started to be on my mind, and I begged to have food brought to me. The nurses never allowed it, but they made sure I was as comfortable as possible. I was getting my nutrients through my IV, and I would doze off and on. My husband was great; he never left my side. He made sure to get me anything needed to get me through this difficult time.

Chapter 3

The Delivery

The very next morning it was time. I went into labor! I woke up with a really strong pain, and I was crying out. The nurse came to check on me, and then they started to prepare me for delivery. My husband was asleep in the chair next to me when suddenly he was awoken by my cry and the noise. It was about 6:00 a.m., and everything was happening so fast. He really didn't know what was going on because he was half asleep. But he woke up quickly. The nurses handed him some scrubs and told him to hurry and dress for delivery. He put them on quickly, and we were off to the delivery room. The delivery room was very cold and bright. I remember the pain growing stronger and stronger, and I was not able to have anything for the pain. I was having a normal birth, so no pain medicine was allowed because it was too late. The doctor told me to push, so I did. I started to push and push, and soon after a baby girl was born weighing 1lb. 5oz. Everything happened rather quickly. I remember my husband wanted to see the baby right away, but I was afraid. I told him not to look at her because I didn't know what to expect. We finally saw her briefly, and she was so beautiful. Even though she was born so early, her body was in perfect condition.

I never got to hold her because the doctor and nurses all rushed her out of the room and into the neonatal intensive care unit. I wasn't allowed to see her again until that night.

I was taken back to my room to rest. My husband was by my side when I woke up, along with the nurses who quickly began to tend to me. They came in and examined me, checked my IV, and made sure I was comfortable. They even let me place my dinner order. My husband and I were left alone in the room once the nurses had finished tending to me. He was so sweet. He gave me a big hug, and we both began to thank God. We thanked God for a fast and good delivery. We had no complications, and it was really quick. We thanked him for his protection and for our baby girl. This time somehow brought us closer to each other, and we were feeling very blessed to have one another. If I needed anything at all, my husband was there. He helped me in and out of bed and with medications; he even brought me some popsicles that the hospital had for the patients. He helped me with dinner, and we began to talk about our baby girl. We realized that we hadn't even named her! Everything had happened so quickly and unexpectedly that we didn't even have a name picked out yet!

Chapter 4

First Visit with Our Baby

My husband carefully wheeled me down to the neonatal intensive care unit (NICU) area in a wheelchair because I was still in too much pain to walk around. When we arrived, the nurse had us sign in and then buzzed us in through the door into the area where our baby was. She then went over all the hospital's guidelines and had us wash and scrub up to our elbows with surgical soap for two to three minutes under warm water. This was expected every time we came to visit our baby. When I saw her for the first time, I couldn't believe my eyes! She was so tiny and perfect; her fingers and toes were so little. Her eyes were covered with a little mask to keep them protected from the light. She was in a small baby bed with tubes and wires all over her feet, hands, and chest. The wires were connected to machines next to her. The machines monitored her pulse, heart rate, and breathing. Another machine helped her breathe; it had a tube that went down into her mouth and lungs. The last tube was a small one inserted into her belly button to help with feeding. It broke my heart to see her that way. How I wished I could just hold her and make her all better. I began to cry and blame myself, thinking *maybe if I had taken better care of myself this wouldn't have happened.* All kinds of thoughts flooded my mind. I felt so guilty because I had worked while I was pregnant. I told my husband how I was feeling, and he comforted me. He assured me that it wasn't my fault; after all, I couldn't help that I had gotten that infection, but I still wished I could have held my baby. My husband very sweetly told me that God was holding our baby, and I knew he was.

The nurse came to tell us that it was time to do tests on our baby, so it was time for us to leave for now. She handed us a picture of our baby that was taken in the NICU with a Polaroid camera. It was so cute! My husband and I then left the NICU and headed back to my room to rest. I got into my hospital bed and turned on the television to keep my mind from wandering. Suddenly my husband came to me and showed me the picture of our baby and said, "So what should we name her"? I smiled as I looked at the picture and thought, *That's right, we have to name her. But what would be a good name?* I looked at my baby in the picture. She was tiny, perfect in color, and a fighter. Suddenly, it came to me, and I asked my husband, "What do you think about the name Ashleigh?" He smiled and said, "It's perfect!" He immediately called down to the NICU and told the nurse that we had named our baby. My husband had thought of her name spelled differently than the tradition way, and he helped the nurse spell it. He was very happy that he thought of the spelling all by himself. If it were up to me, I would have spelled it the traditional way. I was just happy with the name Ashleigh. What a beautiful name for a beautiful baby girl!

Chapter 5

Ashleigh's Stay in the NICU

After I had given birth to Ashleigh, I stayed in the hospital for two more days before I had to leave her. When it was time to actually leave, it was very hard for me. It was as if a part of me was missing, and I cried and cried. What made it more difficult was that my husband and I weren't able to visit Ashleigh before we left. It seemed like the NICU nurses always had to take tests and perform blood transfusions on Ashleigh.

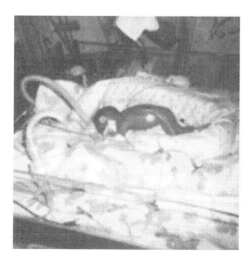

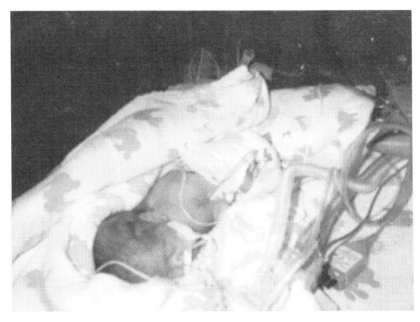

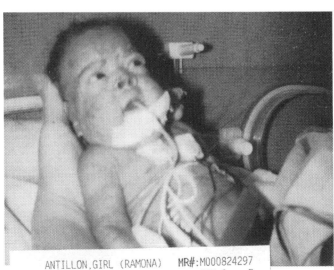

ANTILLON,GIRL (RAMONA)   MR#:M000824297
NICU   DOB: 05/27/01 Age: 00M Sex: F
Att Dr: Tisdell,Scott Christopher
Acct #: V00006809214 ADM Date: 05/27/01

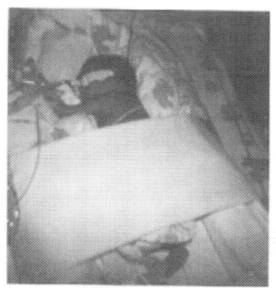

Ashleigh Renée Antillon
1 month + 4 days

We were allowed to see Ashleigh as much as possible, or as much as the doctor and nurses allowed us. Every time we wanted to see Ashleigh, we had to call the NICU before heading out because if a new baby was being admitted or if tests we're being done then we couldn't visit. At first I understood, but then as the days passed I began to feel upset. Ashleigh was my baby; shouldn't I have the right to see her when I wanted? I was an emotional wreck. It seemed like the doctor and nurses were always working on Ashleigh or admitting a new baby when I wanted to see her. I knew that they were only doing what was best for Ashleigh, but it was still very difficult.

For the first week her condition was what doctors called the *honeymoon stage*. This meant that Ashleigh would appear fine for a week then go downhill soon after. That's when we first got the bad news. The doctor was so cold and heartless when he called. He called to tell us that Ashleigh's lungs were deteriorating and she might not make it through the night. My heart sank, and I began to cry. What made it worse was that my husband and I couldn't see Ashleigh at the time. We had to wait until the nurses were ready for us. They would call us once all the tests and procedures were done. When we were finally allowed to see Ashleigh, the doctor explained her treatment to us. She was given steroids to help with her lungs and breathing. Ashleigh had made it through the night, and we were so thankful. She still got infection after infection along with several blood transfusions, but she was well taken care of. The nurses treated the infections without knowing where they came from, but soon they found out that the infections were coming from a tube they called the central line. That tube was inserted in Ashleigh's mouth and went down into her stomach. An X-ray was taken to make sure that it was in the right place and would help feed Ashleigh. Although it helped with her feeding, it had to be removed. An incision was made on the right side of her rib cage, and the tube was now inserted there so she could get her food and medicines. The doctors thought it would be best if Ashleigh was on breast milk, and she was for a while, until I ran out of milk. The doctor now decided he would have to put Ashleigh on store milk. Now finding the right one was another story. Since her stomach was so delicate, the doctor tried four different kinds of milk before he found the one that wouldn't make her spit up or give her an infection. The nurses actually showed my husband and me a green fluid that was drawn out of the tube from her stomach. The green fluid indicated to the doctor and nurses that there was an infection due to the milk that was being used. Ashleigh would gain weight but then lose it every time they stopped her feeding tube. Soon after, thanks to God and much prayer, the doctor discovered the right kind of milk, called Similac Neosure. She began to gain weight and keep it on with no more infections.

The next three months were still very hard, and we faced many different obstacles. The worst one of all was when she had head bleeds. The doctor called us and told us that she had a head bleed on her right side. It was called a grade A head bleed, which usually resolves itself. It did, but then she got another head bleed on the left side. This time it was called a grade 2, which is a lot more dangerous than the first one. It could either get better or get worse; there was no way to treat it. If it got worse, she would be mentally challenged. However, thanks to God and much prayer, the head bleed was gone, and the bleeding caused no brain damage. Then there was the time I called the NICU to see if I could visit Ashleigh, and the nurse said that it wasn't a good time. She went on to explain that when changing the tubes another nurse on duty hadn't use adhesive remover when taking off the tape around Ashleigh's mouth causing a big tear on the right side of her ear. I was furious. I immediately had my husband take me to the hospital. When we arrived, we had to wait to see Ashleigh. Finally we were allowed to see her, and the tear was covered with four little strips. The tear soon got better, but it left a good-size scar next to her ear. Soon after, things began to get better with Ashleigh. She began to grow bigger and stronger with each passing day.

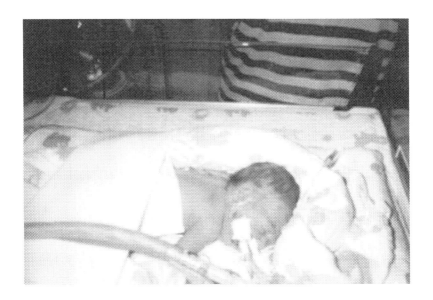

We kept our church family informed about Ashleigh and her condition. My husband and I had attended Harvest Temple Church in Grand Prairie, Texas, since we were married in 1998. The church was by our side through every good and bad report. Our pastor and the church family were wonderful. They offered prayer, support, and lots of their own time to visit Ashleigh at the hospital. One very sweet woman by the name of Patty Carreon, who also attended Harvest Temple with us, came to see Ashleigh one morning. She handed me a poem that the Lord inspired her write for Ashleigh.

Ashleigh Renea Antillon

I sent you to earth early before you were due
For I wanted the world to see my hand upon you
Ashleigh, you are a miracle child and people will know
That my love, mercy, and grace on you I have bestowed
For you will grow and you will seek Me by choice
I will be your strength and I will bless your voice
I have summoned you and called you by name
You will remind everyone that I am the God who reigns
I will do signs and miracles to all those who believe in Me
By accepting my Son, Jesus, I will welcome them into eternity
Because of your miracle birth, people will come to understand
I am the Giver of Life and have made you with my own hands
People will be amazed at your size and they will find
I have breathed life in you, and you will grow stronger with time
No one will doubt that I am the God of all Flesh; they will see
Is there anything too hard for Me?
Because of your premature birth, I wanted everyone to see
My miracle child you have come to be

Isaiah 45:1-8

An Inspirational Poem by Patty Carreon
May 27, 2001

I read that poem every night, and it encouraged me. I knew without a doubt that Ashleigh was meant to be here with us early and that there was nothing too hard for God!

Chapter 6

The First Time I Held Ashleigh

The day finally came when I could hold Ashleigh for the first time. I was scared at first because there were so many wires and she was so small. I was handed a gown to wear that opened up at the front, and I was soon able to get comfortable as I reclined on a chair to hold her. The gown allowed her to lie on my bare chest so she could learn my scent and get used to me. The doctor and nurses called it a *kangaroo hug*. This would help Ashleigh feel loved and know that I was her mommy. Ashleigh had never been held, and she needed to get used to being out of her bed and being held. It took some getting used to, but it was all worth it. Soon she just lay there sleeping comfortably. She felt so soft. I held her for hours; then I had to put her back to bed. For the next several weeks we visited Ashleigh, and I had lots of kangaroo hugs with her. Before long, she knew that I was her mommy and that she was much loved.

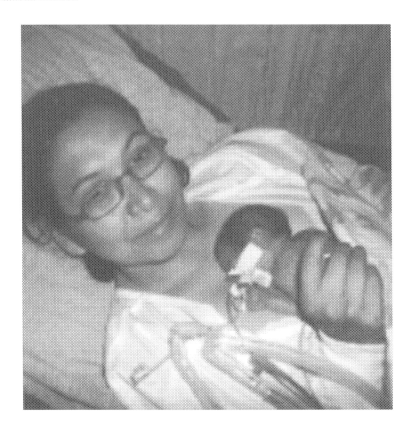

7-17-01 5:40pm
First time Mona holds Ashleigh

In September the doctor told my husband and I that Ashleigh would need eye surgery or she would be blind. At first I didn't want to allow the surgery. I told my husband that God would heal her eyes without having to have surgery. My husband soon convinced me that we needed to allow the surgery and doing so didn't mean that we weren't trusting in God. He went on to explain that God had placed the doctors there so he could work through them and give Ashleigh's eye the proper care. I then agreed to have the surgery, and it was scheduled for later that week. My husband and I arrived at the hospital about 6:00 a.m.

We were allowed to see Ashleigh briefly before the surgery. The nurse had to begin preparing her for surgery, so we soon had to leave for the waiting area. As we waited it seemed like it was taking forever for the doctor to come and let us know anything. The surgery lasted two and a half hours, and then the doctor finally came in and told us that the surgery was a success. He explained that we had the surgery just in time to correct her eyes but that she still might need to wear glasses in the future. We were so happy and relieved that it all went well. We thanked God once again for having his hand upon Ashleigh. We didn't mind the possibility of her wearing glasses in the future; after all, she had her eyesight. We were then able to see her once she was back in the NICU. As I looked at her sleeping, I saw a mask over her eyes to protect them from the light, and she looked perfect. I thought to myself, *wow, God is a good God!* We visited with Ashleigh for an hour before we had to leave.

Chapter 7

Ashleigh's Last Month in the NICU

During the next couple of weeks, we still visited Ashleigh as much as the NICU allowed us. Then the day came when Ashleigh didn't have a tube to help with her feedings and she was placed in an incubator. I was able to feed her by myself. I was given a tiny bottle to use at her feedings. The bottle only had four ounces of milk at one feeding, and I had to burp Ashleigh for every two ounces she drank. It was so cute. She was growing bigger and doing so well with every passing day. Once the doctor realized how good she was doing, he decided to move her to a regular crib-like bed to sleep for the rest of her stay in the NICU. She still needed the monitor, but she no longer needed the breathing machine. The monitor kept an eye on her heart rate. It was just a belt wrapped around her chest and was easy to remove for bathing and changing. The nurses began to allow me to bathe her myself. I was very scared and nervous because she was still small. I used a bucket the size of a sink, and after a few practices I was comfortable bathing and dressing her. I was a pro and ready to take her home. The doctor told my husband and me that we would have to take a CPR class and stay the night in the hospital with Ashleigh before we could take her home. The hard part was about to begin.

We arrived at the hospital on September 11, 2001, exhausted from preparing the house for her arrival. We met the teacher of the CPR class just in time. As we started the class, the teacher went over one more detail we would have to learn. She went over the use of the monitor that Ashleigh wore around her chest. The monitor would indicate when Ashleigh's heart rate was low or if she stopped breathing. We also learned how to assemble the monitor after a bath or changing. I had it all together until the nurse came in to drop off Ashleigh and go over all her medication. My husband and I were not prepared at all. We had dropped off Ashleigh's prescriptions at the pharmacy the hospital recommended, and several of them would not be ready until morning. This was really bad because Ashleigh needed them through the night. Thankfully, the hospital had plenty of her medicine to spare and gave us some to use until my husband could go to the pharmacy in the morning. The nurse explained the way the medicines needed to be measured and poured in her bottle; she even had everything written down on a sheet of paper. It wasn't easy, but we finally got it right. The nurse then left my husband and me alone to care for Ashleigh, and I was faced with caring for Ashleigh without the help of the nurses. I soon became scared and upset. I went through so many different emotions because there was so much information to take in and her medication had to be given at certain times. I felt like I couldn't handle it all by myself. My husband then assured me that he would be there to help me out and that I wasn't alone. He was very helpful with Ashleigh for the rest of the night, and I soon felt better and ready to take her home.

Chapter 8

Ashleigh Comes Home

My husband and I made it through the night with Ashleigh, and when morning came we were so excited to be leaving the hospital. All the nurses and her doctor came in to say good-bye to her; it was very emotional. This had been Ashleigh's home for the past three and a half months, and the nurses had grown attached to her. They invited us to bring Ashleigh back every year in September for the annual NICU reunion that was held at the hospital. It was a chance for the nurses and doctors to keep in touch with how Ashleigh was doing, and so we agreed to come. As for the doctor who had been so cold and heartless from the beginning, well, he had a different feeling now. He stood over Ashleigh, smiled, and said, "God is surely on her side." Then he said good-bye and walked out of the room. I was amazed how even he couldn't deny the hand of God on Ashleigh's life. I thought to myself, *How awesome, my little baby is a living testimony of God's goodness.*

My husband and I prepared to leave the room. We strolled Ashleigh out very carefully and loaded her in the car to finally take her home. When we arrived at home my husband was very helpful with Ashleigh and her things. He still had to go pick up our other two children from their grandma's house, so he just dropped us off and made sure that we were all settled. I wanted the kids to be surprised to see Ashleigh since they were never allowed to see her in the NICU. At the time they were one and six, too young to visit her. I was nervous about what their reaction would be to finally have Ashleigh home. I sat on the edge of the bed holding Ashleigh in my arms when suddenly I heard my husband arrive with the kids. My husband and kids walked in so surprised they couldn't believe their eyes. Daniel did well with Ashleigh. It was Abrianna who made me cry. Ashleigh was only four pounds twelve ounces, so she looked like a baby doll. My husband told Abrianna, "Look, it's your baby." So Abrianna thought it was her doll. She began to laugh then cry. She wanted to hold Ashleigh but would pull away when Ashleigh would move or cry. It was as if she couldn't believe that a baby so tiny was moving and crying. So she just stayed close to my husband. As for Daniel, he was very happy to have her home with us, and he started to love on her and wanted to help me do anything to help with her. After watching Daniel be so helpful with Ashleigh, Abrianna soon wanted to help out too. They both did so well with her arrival.

Chapter 9

Challenges Caring for Ashleigh

My husband and I now had a very important job that would take the both of us. Ashleigh had six different kinds of medicines to take several times a day, so my husband decided to arrange all them in order for me. He boiled and washed all her bottles, nipples, and lids. He then measured, labeled, and placed all her medicines in order in boxes. There were five to six syringes of one kind of medicine in each box so that there would be a lot of medicines ready for use. He even stayed up really late to make a schedule for her medicines to make sure I gave them to her on time, just like at the hospital. All this was very helpful, but taking care of Ashleigh was very challenging because she was used to the way the nurses had taken care of her for those three and a half months. For example, I couldn't love on her too much or help her with a bottle. She pulled away when I tried to feed her and would cry nonstop until I put her down. It was as if she was not used to being away from the hospital and the nurses. For those three and a half months those nurses were like her moms because they spent more time with Ashleigh than I did. This made it really hard to get close to Ashleigh. I did everything I could to make Ashleigh comfortable. I sang to her, cradled her, and bathed and rocked her. Nothing helped. I found myself feeling depressed and unsure of my feelings for her. During the first few weeks of having her home, I felt like I was going through postpartum depression. My mother-in-law was there for me, and I expressed how I felt. She quickly began to encourage me and pray for me, and I soon felt a lot better. I began to notice that when I put Ashleigh down she would stop crying, so I would just hold her for a little while then put her down to make her comfortable. When it was time to feed her, I would just place her in her car seat so she could feed herself. It would take her an hour just to drink two ounces of milk. I used a blanket to prop up the bottle as she drank the milk. Then I would burp her when it was time. Now, bedtime was tricky. I had to make sure that her arms and legs were wrapped nice and snug, the same way the nurses in the NICU would do for her. I soon figured out that I had to use the same methods that were used in the NICU in order to make her happy. I always had her eyes covered with a thin blanket to shield her eyes while she slept. I used her blanket to keep her pacifier in her mouth because she couldn't keep it in her mouth by herself and the pacifier helped her fall asleep.

Then there were the breathing treatments that I had to give her three times a day. I did them every morning, noon, and night. Those treatments helped her breathe, and they also helped her during the cold season. And finally I had to deal with the monitor. I had a really hard time with it. It was wrapped around her chest, and I only took it off at bath time or to change clothes. It had wires that needed to be placed correctly otherwise it would make a really loud, horrible noise, like an alarm. One time the alarm wouldn't stop making that noise, and it gave my husband and me quite the scare. It happened right when Ashleigh had finished her bottle. She had an acid reflex problem, and the doctor had her on a certain kind of reflex medicine to help her stomach digest the milk. I had to make sure that I gave Ashleigh this medicine fifteen minutes before her feedings. If I didn't wait the fifteen minutes, she would start choking and having trouble breathing. When that would happen, the monitor would go off. I would have to suction out her mouth and nose because the milk would come out, making Ashleigh gasp for air.

Then there was one morning when she turned blue, and the monitor kept going off. I decided to take her to see her doctor. Luckily we took her just in time. It turned out that Ashleigh had a decreased amount of oxygen. Her doctor quickly called for an ambulance to take her to the hospital because the amount kept dropping. The ambulance came and rushed Ashleigh to the hospital, and I stayed with Ashleigh in a room while she was being treated. The hospital decided to admit Ashleigh due to her oxygen level not being high enough. We were then taken to a regular room where the doctors could continue to treat Ashleigh and get her oxygen level back to normal. I began to be so frustrated with the nurses. They never let Ashleigh sleep because they kept checking on her, and they wouldn't allow me to take care of her the way I wanted to. That made it difficult for Ashleigh because she had become used to my way of caring for her. One of the things the nurses didn't allow was for Ashleigh to be bundled up as she slept. They also didn't allow her to have anything covering her eyes to shield the light, which caused Ashleigh to cry most of the night. Even though I tried to explain to them why she was uncomfortable and crying, they still didn't allow it. She ended up needing to stay there for a little over a week. It was very hard for both Ashleigh and me. She had to have several oxygen treatments, X-rays, and medication before her oxygen level was back to normal. The hospital finally discharged Ashleigh, and we headed back home. I followed up with Ashleigh's primary-care physician as scheduled on a monthly basis, and with God's help, it became easier to care for Ashleigh with each passing day. Soon all medicines and feeding schedules became so natural to me, and we grew very close to each other. We played together, and I sang to her. Even though I couldn't sing, she loved it! I pampered her at bath time. I would lotion and powder her all up, cleaning her ears, and then carefully dressing her. I had to use a comb on her hair because she had so little hair. It was so cute. I loved every moment of it.

Chapter 10

Visits to the Specialty Doctors

As months passed, Ashleigh still needed to see specialty doctors. She had to see lung and kidney specialists along with a neurologist. They were all located in Fort Worth, Texas, at Cook Children's Hospital, not exactly close to us. Ashleigh's great grandfather and a great man of God, Raymond Martinez, helped me take her to see all her specialty doctors. Even though they were far, he still offered to take me every time. He was the most wonderful man and grandfather and great-grandfather to all his grandchildren and great-grand babies, especially to my Ashleigh. His eyes would light up every time he saw Ashleigh. He'd always make her smile as he played with her while we were in the waiting room. He would blow her kisses and say, "She is so precious!" With so many doctor visits, he was such a big help with Ashleigh.

The very first doctor we took Ashleigh to visit was the lung specialist. He listened to her lungs and prescribed the breathing medication along with steroids to help her lungs. Next was her kidney specialist. Ashleigh saw him for medication to help her kidneys function properly as well as for tests. She had to do a few tests and then she was all done; it seems that the medication she had been taking since birth had really helped. Finally, there was the neurologist. This meant more tests for Ashleigh. The test would let the doctor know how her nervous system was developing. She had a little trouble with her mobility, so he suggested I call a physical therapist. He also said that he'd make Ashleigh's primary-care doctor aware of the need. We visited these specialty doctors every three to six months. Everything went well with each visit. The lung specialist continued to prescribe breathing medication during allergy and cold seasons. His close attention to Ashleigh's lungs was great; the kidney and neurologist doctors were great too. They performed the proper tests on Ashleigh and knew how much medicine she needed. With every visit they would lower the amount of medication she had been taking.

Chapter 11

Therapy for Ashleigh

Ashleigh was doing great! All I needed now was to find her a regular therapist to help with her mobility. I mentioned to her primary-care doctor about the physical therapy that Ashleigh needed, and she recommended I call Early Childhood Intervention, also known as ECI. I called ECI, and right away I had a physical therapist scheduled to come out to evaluate Ashleigh. The physical therapist that came out was Emily Young, and she was great with Ashleigh. The first visit was to talk about Ashleigh's history from birth and to gather all of her information so that the therapist could determine what methods were best for Ashleigh. The therapist felt that it was important to start seeing Ashleigh right away and scheduled times to meet with her. She came to our house three days a week to help Ashleigh with her mobility. Ashleigh was three months behind on doing things that babies her age were already doing, which made it challenging for the therapist. Ashleigh definitely had a lot of catching up to do. The therapist was great and so patient with her. She worked with little ones all the time, so she understood that being born as early as twenty-three weeks was going to be more difficult than most babies she had worked with.

From the start of therapy, Ashleigh had trouble doing the simply things, such as making different sounds and noises, turning, and moving her arms and hands. She even needed help sitting, keeping her head up while sitting, and lifting herself up from a lying down position. She couldn't grasp or hold onto things at all. With all the therapy she was going to need, her therapist knew exactly what methods to use to help Ashleigh's mobility. For starters, she brought along a bag of toys that made different sounds and had colorful lights. She also brought a pillow that wrapped around Ashleigh to help her sit by herself. She did several exercises to strengthen Ashleigh's muscles. One of the exercises was having Ashleigh lie down and then she would pull Ashleigh up from her arms, making her do a sit-up. The second one was having Ashleigh reach for a toy and release it; this took a while but she finally got the hang of it. The third one was using patterns and shapes along with lighted toys and having Ashleigh follow them, not only with her eyes, but by turning and using her head and body as well. I remember watching how well Ashleigh would do from visit to visit. On the days the therapist didn't come, I even worked with her on my own, doing the same things the therapist did.

Over the course of six months, Ashleigh made significant improvement. She made all kinds of different sounds and rolled around like crazy. She could grasp and hold her toys, she could sit up on her own, and she could move her arms and hands without looking so stiff. She started to crawl and even wanted to start walking. What a difference from the beginning of her therapy. One habit that Ashleigh had as a result of the therapy was one of my favorite habits. Her mind was trained so well with patterns and colors that everything, and I do mean everything, had to be in the correct spot; nothing could be out of place. She still saw her therapist for two more years but had very few visits. Her therapist came twice a month to make sure that she kept track of Ashleigh's activities as she was growing. When Ashleigh was two years old, her therapist recommended I take Ashleigh to see a speech teacher before she turned three to help with her verbal skills. Ashleigh was doing awesome with her mobility but now needed help talking. Now I had to find a good speech teacher. I put it in God's hands to help me find the right one.

Chapter 12

No More Medicines for Ashleigh

I continued to follow up with Ashleigh's specialty doctors to keep her healthy. Ashleigh visited the kidney specialist regularly, and with each visit he lowered her medication. Finally in 2002, after performing several tests, he felt that she no longer needed medication to help with her kidneys and released her from his care. Also in 2002, the neurologist was so impressed with Ashleigh's mobility and improvement that he stopped all her medication and felt that she didn't need to continue seeing him. We visited the lung specialist as usual until 2003 when he too felt that Ashleigh no longer needed medication, and he released her from his care. Ashleigh was growing and eating well, and with the good reports from the specialty doctors, her primary-care doctor felt that it was not necessary to follow up with any more specialty doctors. She even took Ashleigh off all her other medicines.

God helped my husband and I through all the long hours of making sure that the medicines were given to her properly. From that time things were looking great. We could now take care of Ashleigh without the worry over giving her the proper medicines at the proper time. I had rarely taken her to a babysitter because I didn't feel confident that her medicines would be given to her properly. What a relief it was for me when she was finally off all the medications; I could now easily let family and friends watch her. Ashleigh was a happy little girl, growing big and strong all because of God!

Chapter 13

Speech Class for Ashleigh

At age three Ashleigh still needed help with her speech, and she was now able to see a speech teacher. I had prayed for God's help, and he did. The school that my younger kids attended was right down the street, and one day as I was picking them up, I met a teacher there who specialized in speech therapy. We began to talk about Ashleigh, and she told me that the school offered a program that Ashleigh could attend at the school. I was so excited. God had answered my prayer once again. I immediately made the necessary arrangements to have Ashleigh enrolled in the school's speech class. She would only go for a couple of hours a week. So it wasn't going to be like attending school full time, but it still had many benefits for her. Ashleigh understood that her big brother and sister went to school every morning, and she was excited when I told her that she would also be going to school with them. My husband and I were happy that she took the news so well. We took her shopping right away. She loved Care Bears, and everything had to be Care Bears. We went looking for a backpack that was just the right size for her. She was still petite and needed a very small backpack to fit her. We searched and searched several different stores before we finally found the perfect size; it was Care Bears. We had purchased everything she needed, and she was ready for her first day of speech class.

On the morning of that first day, Ashleigh was so cute and ready for school. I dressed her in a purple outfit, and I fixed her hair, giving her two ponytails on the sides of her head. Her hair was still thin and short, so her ponytails were very small and curly. When we arrived at the school, her speech teacher, Mrs. High, greeted us. She had been expecting Ashleigh that morning to show her to her new classroom. I watched Ashleigh as I left, and she did quite well with Mrs. High. She smiled and waved bye. She was a big girl now. I was sad to leave her, but I knew that this was best thing for Ashleigh and that she would do great. When it came time to pick up Ashleigh, I was so excited as I waited in the hallway for her. I couldn't wait to hear how her first day went and all the things she did. Mrs. High opened the door and escorted Ashleigh out. Ashleigh had the biggest smile on her face. She came over to me and gave me a big hug and kiss on the cheek. Her teacher talked with me about all the different things that Ashleigh learned that day and said that she had a great first day. As Ashleigh attended school in the following weeks, her teacher expressed to me the different goals she wanted Ashleigh to reach by the end of the school year. She expressed that Ashleigh was off to a good start and that she was looking forward to working with her.

It was very helpful having Ashleigh in speech class. It made her have a more outgoing personality. Normally, Ashleigh was a very quiet and shy little girl and didn't talk much. Even with us at home, she got her point across mainly by pointing and making sounds to get the things she needed or wanted. She never had conversations with anyone, including us, so speech class was great for Ashleigh. Mrs. High worked very hard with Ashleigh over the course of that first year, helping her with her verbal skills. She used flash cards with words that were in big letters, making it easier for Ashleigh to see. She used colors, numbers, and patterns and had Ashleigh mix and match items. She would have homework assignments for Ashleigh, and as I helped her with them, I could see how well she was learning. I was so impressed by how well Ashleigh was doing in speech class; she had definitely reached and passed all of Mrs. High's goals. I started to notice that she would say more words when asking for things. She would say things out of the blue and knew how to use words in sentences; she would even have conversations with the family! Even though Ashleigh was born so early and developed at a slower pace than most children, her mind was amazing. It was like a sponge soaking up all the different information and then putting it to use in everyday activities.

Ashleigh continued attending speech class even as she entered pre-K and kindergarten. She was taken out of class on Tuesday and Thursday for about thirty minutes to work on different verbal exercises. Test scores showed that she needed a little more help. Ashleigh ranked in a lower percentage bracket, and her teacher needed her to rank higher, according to state regulations. Several tests were given to Ashleigh throughout the school years, and by the middle of her kindergarten year she passed all the different tests given to her and ranked in the higher percentage bracket, according to the state regulations.

Chapter 14

Normal Everyday Life with Ashleigh

Every new day was an enjoyable one with Ashleigh. What began as an unexpected delivery, we now saw as a wonderful blessing. We always called her our miracle baby. She overcame all those obstacles, from having tubes and wires everywhere in her body to needing help to eat to getting infections and head bleeds and needing eye surgery, even from needing so many medications and struggling with her mobility and speech. She now enjoys doing what little girls her age do. She has favorite television shows. She loves to play outside with her sister and enjoys swinging on the swing and swimming. She has grown very close to her big sister Abrianna; they do everything together.

Ashleigh now has a new baby brother. She's a big sister and is great with him. Ashleigh's heart is so full of love for everyone; she is indeed our miracle child. She's so sweet, loving, and thoughtful to others and always does what she is told. If she is told to share with her brothers and sister, she will. She will help clean up messes that she didn't even make just to be helpful to her sister and baby brother. Everything she does is with excellence. When learning how to ride a bike or learning new things, she keeps trying until she figures it out. The day she wanted to ride her bike without the training wheels, she tried and tried it until she finally succeeded. She never gives up on anything; she has a habit of finishing everything she starts, big or small. She's amazing! One time my husband and I took the kids to the park, and we watched Ashleigh as she started to go up a rock-climbing obstacle. She then stopped and got down. She circled around the play set and went to play on the slide. Then she came back to the rock climbing part several times and looked at it for a while and then finally started to climb it again until she reached the top. It just bothered her that she couldn't reach the top of it, and she was determined to reach the top that same day. My husband and I later talked and concluded that all of the therapy she had all those years helped develop her personality. It's fun to watch her act like that. It's such a joy having Ashleigh. She keeps us smiling and laughing daily, and we love to see her grow with each passing day.

She loves to go to school and to celebrate—all types of parties, whether it is a holiday party at school or a friend's birthday party or even her own birthday party. I am always happy to help her take goodies to all of the parties. It puts a big smile on Ashleigh's face. A birthday at our house is always a big deal. I use favorite themes for boys or girls with every party and have matching colors, balloons, and cake. I make a lot food and have games and prizes. I even have a matching piñata and candy bags that match to give to each of our guests. I make sure to go all out; everyone always has a great time. Every birthday for Ashleigh is so special to our family and friends because when we look at Ashleigh blow out her candles, we see God's miracle baby—a life that doctors and nurses didn't believe would make it, a life that has overcome so many obstacles and struggles so early in life. A life that God used to show everyone how powerful his hand really is *when* you trust in him with all your heart!

Chapter 15

Glasses for Ashleigh

Then the day came when Ashleigh needed to wear glasses. I noticed that Ashleigh was having trouble seeing things far away and that she had to sit up close to watch television. The school nurse had performed a vision test, and Ashleigh failed it. That's when I knew that I should take her to see her doctor. At the doctor we went over the history of her eye surgery, and the doctor referred us to an eye specialist to examine Ashleigh's eyes better. This was on December 20, 2005; the doctor was Michael G. Hunt. On the day of the visit, I discussed with the doctor all of Ashleigh's past medical conditions and the laser eye surgery performed at the hospital. He gave Ashleigh a vision screen test from his office, and she failed that one, too. He then examined her eyes to see the result of her having the laser surgery. The examination went well; her retina was normal. He did, however, find that Ashleigh had moderate myopia and significant astigmatism, more on her left eye than her right. He felt that glasses would help her, so he prescribed her a pair. He scheduled a checkup in six to eight weeks to reexamine her eyesight and to see if the glasses he prescribed had corrected the problem. If at that time he still saw a problem then he would have to start her on amblyopia treatment.

Right away I took Ashleigh to Walmart to have the prescription for her new glasses filled. She was pretty excited once she saw all the different colors and styles the store had. She wanted blue glasses, and she found some really cute light-blue ones. She got measured and fit for the ones she picked out and had to wait a week for them to be ready. She couldn't wait for them to come in; she would ask me every day if the glasses were ready yet. Finally, after a week Walmart called me to pick up her glasses. I immediately took Ashleigh to pick up her glasses; she could hardly wait to have them. She was so happy when we arrived at the store and tried on the glasses. She smiled at herself in the mirror and said, "I can see good!" On the way back home she pointed out everything she saw; it was so cute. This made me very happy because I knew that she was able to see things clearly now.

At school Ashleigh did great when it came to seeing things in the classroom. When she had trouble in class, she kept at it until she got it right. She was the class helper and loved it. I noticed that having her new glasses gave her confidence to do everything in school and at home. I took Ashleigh back to visit the eye doctor as scheduled, and the visit went well. The doctor examined her eyes; everything looked good with her new glasses. There was no need to start the amblyopia treatment. I continue to follow up with the eye doctor every six months to take care of any changes in her vision or if there was any need for eye drops. Having glasses for her isn't a bad thing at all, and she looks so cute in them.

As time passes, I hold on to all of the words mentioned in the poem given to Ashleigh by Patty Carreon. I remember one part in particular where it talked about God blessing her voice. I noticed that all that was spoken in the poem came to pass, but this one part about Ashleigh's voice now comes to mind when I notice how much she love music. Ashleigh will sing in the car, at home, and in school concerts. She even sings in church programs, and she's pretty good. I buy her music every chance I get so she can listen to it in her room at home. She was shy at first, but little by little she began to open up to singing in front of people during plays. Now she'll sing her heart out.

We attend church, and she loves to learn about Jesus. I bought her a child's Bible made of a bear and she always has it during prayer time at night and at church. I see how much she loves God and how she wants to know more and more about him. That's when I remember all the promises God mentioned in the poem for Ashleigh!

Chapter 16

Ashleigh Now

Well, it's now been nine and a half years since Ashleigh was born. We have always taken her to the Neonatal Intensive Care Unit reunions. They're always so much fun and different every year. The whole family has made it an annual tradition that we look forward to. It's always the fourth Thursday in September; we receive an invitation in the mail for it. For that day I always like to make Ashleigh feel extra special; I tell her it's her party we're going to. I buy her a really pretty outfit and matching shoes, and I style her hair very pretty. I do all of this so that when she takes pictures we can see how much she's changed through the years and so we have lasting memories. The hospital always goes all out for the kids that day too. They have many cool games and prizes. There's fresh fruit, cake, and punch, and they take pictures of everyone. On Ashleigh's eighth visit she won a twenty-five-dollar gift card to Barnes & Noble. She loves to read, so she was so happy to have a gift card for a bookstore. Ashleigh has grown up to be big and strong and very smart. She loves to read, write, and do math problems, even when she's away from school. She made the A honor roll this year in the fourth grade. My husband and I are so proud of her. She can do anything she puts her mind and heart to; my husband and I noticed this way back when she was so young. What a blessing God has given us!

My husband has been coaching our older daughter Abrianna's softball team, called the "Stars," for two years. Ashleigh now joins in the fun. She never did before because she was too afraid of the ball, but she finally overcame that fear and plays on the team too. She always wanted to, but she needed to feel comfortable with all the rules of the game. So my husband practiced with her at home until one day she agreed to play for the team. He was so happy because now he had both his girls on the team. Abrianna is the team's pitcher, and Ashleigh will play first or outfield, where ever my husband feels that she can play better. She's a good catcher and runner who plays really hard and looks forward to every game. Ashleigh and Abrianna play really well together because they are used to playing with each other at home. When Ashleigh is at first base, she will catch her sister's throws and tag the runner out. The team won first place and were the undefeated team of the season. Not bad for Ashleigh's first season of softball!

She's come a long way from when she first started practicing with my husband. Now she's so comfortable that she's trying to pitch. She has watched my daughter Abrianna pitch for so long that now she wants to try. It looks like it's going to be one of those things that she'll keep at it until she gets it.

Playing softball is only one of the many things Ashleigh enjoys doing. She enjoys music and is interested in instruments, such as the guitar and the piano. For one Christmas I bought her a guitar and a karaoke machine so she could sing. She uses her karaoke machine more than her guitar and hopes to learn how to play the guitar more someday. She really enjoys the piano, and for now it's all about playing music on the piano. We have a piano that she practices on all by herself and enjoys playing in her free time. My husband learned how to play the piano from his father and now has shown Ashleigh how to play. My husband's family is musically talented. My husband knows how to play some of the church hymns as well as a Christmas song, and now Ashleigh has learned to play them too. She is so quick to learn all the songs that my husband has run out of songs to teach her. Now she'll just play what she knows over and over again. I think that she took after my husband's family because of the way she plays the piano. She plays the piano really fast; her fingers will roll over the keys. It's beautiful. Every morning she plays. I love to hear her play all of the songs. My favorite is called "For Thou Oh Lord." She can also play "Friends" by Michael W. Smith, "Lord I Lift Your Name on High," "We Bring a Sacrifice of Praise into the House of the Lord," "Give Them All to Jesus," and "Happy Birthday Jesus." She will play them over and over again. Finally, my father-in-law is teaching her some new songs. She thinks that's neat. My father-in-law even gave her an antique piano on her ninth birthday because he has seen how much she loves to play. The antique piano is special to Ashleigh because it also belonged to her grandmother, who passed away five years ago; now Ashleigh has something that belonged to her grandmother. We placed the piano in the front room of our house. That way Ashleigh will have her own room to play in whenever she wants. She plays the piano every day, and she worships Jesus in the songs she plays.

I hope that she'll continue to play and learn more songs as time passes and maybe sing and play the piano in church one day.

Ashleigh is a happy, healthy little girl who succeeds at everything she does and who loves her family. She will be silly at times and be sad at other times. She loves to watch movies and eat popcorn. Her favorite desert is vanilla ice cream, and she eats it really fast. I tease and say to her that if the family were ever in an ice-cream eating contest, she would win it for us. She's our ice-cream-eating champion! She loves to have slumber parties with friends and read bedtime stories.

She still has to have an eye mask over her eyes in order to sleep. She loves to play dress up with her sister and her friend Mary. She loves praying and kisses at bedtime. All of this would not be possible if it weren't for God. He has a purpose for her life. I thank God every day for my Ashleigh. When I look at her I always remember that *nothing is impossible for God!*

Chapter 17

With God All Things Are Possible

The birth of Ashleigh was indeed a powerful miracle for our family. Although some things we endured did not feel good at the time, I believe they made my faith grow stronger in the Lord. I believe the Lord will never give you more than you can handle and will never leave you during hard times. I reflect a lot on that hard time with Ashleigh. There were days that I felt scared, felt like giving up, and felt like I couldn't do it. But I held on to the Lord, and he was my strength. He showed me time and time again his mighty power and that his hand was on Ashleigh. Now when I go through trying times, I always reflect on God's goodness and that if he was with me then, he'll be with me time and time again.

Everything we go through in life is for a reason and has a purpose. Sometimes a situation may hurt us and we may feel like it's breaking us. But the experience always makes us stronger somehow. We will get through it *if* we put our trust in the Lord. Sometimes it can also be God's divine will for things to happen in a certain way. In Ashleigh's premature birth, there was a reason and purpose; it was God's divine will for it to happen the way it did. Her birth was truly the hardest thing I have ever experienced, but God was there holding my hand every step of the way. Although I didn't feel good when I was going through it, soon after I felt stronger and could say, *Thank you, Jesus for entrusting me with such a great miracle!* God is powerful. It is God who formed Ashleigh and breathed life into her. Every detail of her was perfectly designed by him. God is so awesome and loves us so much more than we can ever imagine. He is there for us when we need him; just call on his name. The name above all other names is Jesus. If you every face a problem that may seem too big, know that it's not. God knows all things and wants us to turn and trust him in everything. You're never alone, even if you feel that you are and that a situation is more than you can handle. Just know that God can and will always do more than you can think or imagine he can do. There is never a situation or problem that is too hard for God. Ashleigh's birth is a testimony to God's goodness, and her life is living proof that *with God all things are possible!*

We all have moments in our lives where we feel alone, like giving up and maybe even

scared at times. On the next few pages I encourage you to write down your

own life experiences. As you reflect on those moments begin to thank God and know

that if he was with you then he will be with you time and time again.

God will never leave you nor forsake you.

God bless you always,
Ramona Antillon

Devotional Journal

_____

_____

_____

_____

_____

_____

There is a friend that sticketh closer than a brother (proverbs 18:24)

Ramona Antillon

_____

_____

_____

_____

_____

_____

The eternal God is thy refuge and underneath are the everlasting
arms . . . .Deuteronomy 33:27

_____

_____

_____

_____

_____

_____

_____

_____

_____

_____

_____

_____

_____

Ramona Antillon

_____

_____

_____

_____

_____

_____

Ramona Antillon

_____

_____

_____

_____

_____

_____

I will never leave thee, nor forsake thee (Hebrews 13:5)

_____

_____

_____

_____

_____

_____

Ramona Antillon

Every word of God is pure; he is a shield unto them that put their trust in him. (Proverbs 30:5)

_____

_____

_____

_____

_____

_____

Enter into his gates with thanksgiving, and into his courts with praise;
be thankful unto him and bless his name. (Psalms 100:4)

Author Biography

I'm a Christian woman who lives in North Texas with my husband of thirteen years and four children. I accepted Jesus Christ in my heart and as my personal savior when I was nineteen years old. He has since been showing me his wonderful love, mercy, and grace. He is forever faithful. I was blessed to have experienced this wonderful miracle birth of our daughter Ashleigh. It has made me stronger in my faith, knowing that God can do all things! I lived through this difficult time and witnessed the hand of God every step of the way. Although there were times I felt scared, he was there holding me and never let me go! When doctors gave me the bad report of how Ashleigh only had a 20 percent chance to live, I placed her in God's hands. Ashleigh is now here with us today, living a normal, happy life. I believe that there is nothing too hard for God. He can do all things!